A PORTER FOLIO

By the same author:

ONCE BITTEN TWICE BITTEN (1961)
POEMS ANCIENT & MODERN (1964)

A
Porter Folio

new poems by

PETER PORTER

SCORPION PRESS

First published in 1969 by
Scorpion Press
Manor House, Pakefield, Lowestoft, Suffolk

ACKNOWLEDGEMENTS

Thanks are due to the editors and publishers of the following periodicals and books in whose pages some of these poems have appeared : *Ambit, Encounter, Isis, The Listener, The London Magazine, New Statesman, The Observer, Oz, Phoenix, The Sunday Times, The Times Literary Supplement, Transatlantic Review,* The Poetry Book Society's *Christmas Supplement 1965,* The Poetry Book Society's *Voice & Verse,* 1965, and *Graffiti,* ed. R. Gordon Freeman, Hutchinson, 1966; and to the British Broadcasting Corporation, in whose programmes *The Poet's Voice* and *Poetry Now* others have been broadcast.

Printed by Villiers Publications Ltd,
Ingestre Road, London, NW5

Dedicated to George MacBeth

CONTENTS

THE LAST OF THE DINOSAURS

Chalky, you've gone —
the only one to see the last
stegosaurus, the blue edged plain
with bald egg-eaters blurring it,
eighty days' rain
before the mating season
and parsley blades neck high —

nice to have known such niceness,
these Cretaceous days!
Tyranno — sore arse — Rex
and other thick necks
thrive. Where's the gentle
ninety ton nonsense
we ate mustard grass beside?

So much time and blue.
That great arc telling
the centuries with its pivotless
movement, tick, tock, tick :
you can watch evolution
in those hairy faces
and poor Protoceratops being sick.

Another gentle day and
nothing to do. When you've lasted
150 million years
you can stand the sound of time.
Some day a mind is going to come
and question all this dance —
I've left footprints in the sand.

Valete and Salvete.
I hear the wintering waters rise
under the hemstitched sky.
Put me in the anthologies,
darling, like Horace almost
killed by a falling tree;
life is a dream or very nearly.

THE THREE DREAMS

The Bird Dream :

> My feet turn out
> so I am a duck,
>> no, a coot and I have a white beak
>> and suggestive walk.
> You're throwing bread on the water,
>> I take a piece from your hand
> and have to waddle over gravel to do it.
>> I'm a floating furnace of love
>> but I'm not adapted to walking.
> You walk away over the pathway
>> and the statue-mounted grass.

The Egg Dream :

> My white is cool
> and slippery
> and nourishing.

> My yoke is rich,
> half-way to red
> and nutty.

> All of me is yours;
> a little bit of me
> is left at the corner
> of your mouth.
> They had to cook me
> before you wanted me.

The Poem Dream :

> If the ink lasts
> this poem will get me finished.

> Not only the ink
> the inspiration must stay the distance.

So I wait my blue epiphany
between phone calls and trips to the kitchen.

You're wearing a mini-skirt
that's well-judged for a girl of thirty,

You're making me on the page
and smile at the pun.

' I was born of an act of love
and now I shall never change '.

THE THIRTEEN COUPLETS

I have found an opening into high self-love
Like a belly full of God in stained glass.

This is one of those parthenogenetic cases,
A new sweet for souls with a self taste.

There are no visions, alas : just as I was getting to know
Dirigibles we start to rendezvous in space.

But I must keep to happiness : happiness is possible
Though there's usually something sexual about it.

Flowers may do and parts of the country
No Liverpool poet has heard of. Joseph Haydn helps.

I thought of a definition : a date with Miss Albion,
The poor chameleon angel led by Blake,

Your small island of torts and friends
Moored somewhere off Radio Caroline,

A sort of Heavenly Donaueschingen
With concrete poets out in dancing pumps

And bewildered bees pulling at plastic flowers
In borders beside pubs with ancient names.

I had heard of your huge sepulchres,
Monuments to Milton and the sweat of stones.

Ah martyrdom, said the colonial, his feet turning out,
This is where they buried Arthur Mee and the remarkable
    things.

There's no art to find the mind's construction in the face,
My enemy and I both love Shakespeare.

But Time reports that God is dead. Long live God.
I am struggling with the pronouns me and my. I am happy,

MY LATE T'ANG PHASE

Unexpected sun on white icing terraces,
Little girls ringing my doorbell and giggling,
More than a lifetime between six o'clock and seven,
Enough loneliness for a novel, enough poise.
Ambition fights talent more than sloth does.
I sit in the warmer, the caramel darkness
Watching two worldly eyes : where is the inseminate
Of boredom, the Rilke of the inflamed will?

Why be beleagured by nerves only?
Why not have tanned historical enemies?
My friends find new forms which make kites
Of confessions : whatever your taste there's
Blood here to back it. I take eight hundred page
Histories of Florence from Paddington Library.
I know nine tabby cats, all pregnant. News?
They dug up the dead who were smiling.

FANTASIA ON A LINE OF STEFAN GEORGE

I shall die if I do not touch your body.
If I cannot claim a small priest-like
Privilege at your waist, my masks
Of face will slip, no tides will work
Your body's shores, no storms rouse
That inland sea. On a hectoring day
I stood in the Natural History Museum
And couldn't breathe. The blue whale
And the passenger pigeon worried for me,
Surely my fingers were losing their prints,
I had no history in my bones, I was
Transparent as a finished gesture.
Where you are is life : this sunlessness
Is only inside my head,
The inverse paradise, rain forest where
Evolution's mother blocked with eggs
Waddles with beak aloft to spin
The thread of fear that leads back to you.

THE BATTLE OF CANNAE

As a great wonder in a world of names
    the child picks Hannibal to be his hero,
outgenerals Rome on the southern grass —
    all day the slaughter lasts, the thrill
radiates to yellow bedroom walls;
    a cell of power is forming in his head
(a model of the battle worth ten
    thousand marks was commissioned by
the German General Staff) : at three o'clock
    in the afternoon it ends; the boy
leaves the Carthaginian panthering,
    takes a sore finger and dislike of sport
into frightening Saturday commonplace.
    To bruise his mind upon the bloody froth
of battles he will expel the air
    from dove-clapped house and sandy street.
No right but clemency can save a life;
    he travels back to find the stretch marks
on history, arrives at the same eclipse
    white-mouthed, informed, explanatory.

AFTER THE TEMPTATION

I come to teach stones
They need not reach for bread;
A thistle carries arms, a sheep's eye
Stands in Heaven for an opal —
Father, the world is only painted on!
No-one's here, I am unprayed by prayer.

I laughed on top of the Temple,
To fall, dog-paddle in God's air,
What are the molecules, the molecules for!
Let that woman die, this bird might lose a wing.
Jump and you can look — Jerusalem
Is always underfoot, when will I be there?

The Travel Agent sent me
Pictures of worlds beyond the piers.
The dogged here has no vacancies,
No boat is leaving. Water returns
The only answer. Father of walls and wharves,
We move. The world is only painted on!

I lead the revolt of iron filings
In the magnetic field.
I am blue and yellow mixed, I am red,
I am God's knees he kneeled in
To kill me, I am dead Abraham,
Dead Isaac, dead star, dead dog dead.

DOROTHY OSBORNE IN THE COUNTRY

Watching the doves in the drowned park,
Every leaf dripping its colourless wax,
The shine of water over the world's face,
I envy the slightest fish in its cold pond.
I shall take the waters of Epsom for my spleen
Among high ladies and their little dogs :
Boredom is like the great clock in the hall,
It writes the hours with unchanging face.

My suitors' wheels turn upon the drive :
Sir Entail and Sir Gravitas approach —
The one owns all a lake and half a shire,
The other is tone deaf and keeps a choir.
The wet birds still sing and dare to love.
Easy to arm against melancholy,
Hard to be true hearted at midnight
Alone in England under uncertain stars.

Fortune is a horse that must be ridden,
Fear a curtain to be pushed aside.
Birds build in soundest branches,
Precepts of love hang all about my eyes.
In a field a boy fights the wind
Whipping his kite to a corner of the sky,
The string still holds and the proud frame
Turns its cheek upon the dangerous air.

A HOPLITE'S HELMET

Inside this helmet
A brain known to great brains

Moved to kill,
The object was in the orders.

The helmetless lover
And boozer fathered as many

New skulls as any,
But he put the helmet back on. You can

Frighten the cat
Poking your fingers through the eye pieces.

When death's eyes
Make a play for me let him approach

In this helmet;
It's sat on some howling scenes —

Witness the old lady
Of Corinth who couldn't be parted

From her sponges;
A yellow bean drying — that was a chunk

Of Epaminondas's brain,
You meet the greatest people in battle.

The helmet's worth
A hundred pounds. Verdigris takes

A month to form
And lasts two thousand years. As many

Million dead
Must come again before this metal dies.

ST. JOHN ON PATMOS

For the right visions
You need a desert or an island.

On an island the beasts will listen,
The groundsel sneak into your cell,

Evil done on the mainland
Will let down a bloody feather at your door,

You get a lion to boss your bestiary
And the best menagerie of all in your head.

What a ramshackle day ! The missed heart beat
Reforms a whole landscape :

That sail is bringing pilgrims, a hymn to God
In your convalesence — the passion-fruit flower

In its sun-suit, heliotrope under the keel
And fish choking in unbreathable blue,

Closer than the enskied artillery of the Lord
Regrettable Emperors with gold hands

And at the right moment of routine
A sure verb to bind the vision to the rock.

Doctors. Doctors. There are things to do.
Kyrie Eleison. But with the world's help.

APPROACHES TO A LINE OF
AUDEN & KALLMAN

Murderer and matron have reached the petits fours,
 Warm wasps are filching our home made jam,
Moons ago honeysuckle wilted at this wall,
 A Telford bridge is inundated by a dam.

Nature relieves herself at the Spastics' Home,
 Sun and righteousness have challenged many,
The tapeworm hatches on a red and rindless world,
 Monsieur Necker died clutching his lucky penny.

Munch, munch, the white ants address the throne,
 Democrats have tempers and renal faults,
The carabinieri are only doing a job,
 Yes, provincials may learn the Metternich waltz.

Brou, brou, like a fire ship comes the bull
 Into a land where even death is kosher;
The fountain of youth throws up new affronts,
 The God Dionysus has entered Bœotia.

FIRST SCENE FROM DOSTOYEVSKY

Whatever quantum of wrong awaits
Its avenger or guilt at the way
That house opens its doors
To the bandaged talkers stirs
The aristocratic lady who
Was rude to a bandsman coming here,
Whatever premonition of nothing
Flashes like a lifted blade
The evening is full of civil music,
The trees are huge with leaf
But will not drop tonight;
Some figures we don't know well
Are promenading down the planted
Lanes. Two of them are quarrelling —
A strain on the others this, yet good
Sense prevails. Only ten minutes before
She was expected, the girl arrives
At her mother's house; half an hour
Early the man picks up his neglected
Book. Someone else is watching.
He has taken up his pen to write :
Not the shot bear or the trapped wolf,
Not the peasant crucified to
His Christ or the madman walking
In blood like snow shall
Assassinate Holy Russia
But men coming in from dances
By moonlight on an evening
With nightingales and women laughing.

SECOND SCENE FROM DOSTOYEVSKY

No sir, this is the patient.
Were you to ask him what
That carriage lamp was,
He'd say a mushroom or
A sticky toffee left under
The seat by a child. He's calm,
Sir, he listens to himself.
There's a man with a flute
Inside his head, his childhood
Plays at Patience with him,
His mother was mauled by a bear —
A ridiculous cliché but
We cannot order our lives.
Beneath his eyelids he has
A map of Pomerania; he'll write
You an essay on Gustavus
Adolphus. We're going
At fifty miles an hour
Through a countryside
Of larches. That other man
In the corner, the one who
Smiles and says nothing,
He may be from Smolensk indeed,
He may also be happy
But he's the man
When we come to the end
Of this journey, in some small
Hotel, probably before dawn,
My friend will kill
And watch with for the first
Light-stepping chambermaid
And the clean light of day.

THE SHINING GOD AND
THE GOD OF CORRECTION

I am haunted, how can I doubt it?
My taxi driver had the face of Anubis,
The thin and fat ladies in their flowing shifts
Passed in and out of doors and were bowed to,
I alone had the glass closed in my face.
Is it my accent, my self deprecation, my race?

I stood by the old sawmill where you said
The reign of felicity would start : I tore
The short leaves of Spring with my nails,
Red sun shone through sawdust but
Ten pigeons could mate while I stood there;
Sensibility capsized on the air.

The yabby diggers were out at four in the morning,
The Shining One stood by a weatherboard house
Dressed in towelling, with roots of grasses
Plaited in his toes. He cherished a dry bone
And watched for dawn to roast the high cloud;
At Eventide Home the wakeful birds were loud.

Death will not save you, said the Corrector,
My mind can penetrate the landlord's formica.
I can work your self-loathing to a fire,
Only your cowardice will help you now :
Grey hairs marshal on your fattening head,
The smell of rotting poems fills your bed.

List the Sullivan operas according to merit,
Write parodies of Gray's two famous Odes,
Arrange Mrs. Beeton as a Cantata text,
Find in Montaigne excuses for getting drunk,
The Watcher with the Code approves these games,
Hell has no faces but many proper names.

Locked in an expanding eye within an eye
The shining world streams out to its end
That's nowhere; it's as short a journey
As to the dirt that glitters at your feet.
Each graded star is polished by the mind,
The all is paraphrased in one line.

An impersonal dream, the kind you don't connect
With your condition : walking among the dead,
Fourteen corpses alone in Station Road,
Colonial architecture, wide verandahs, frangipani,
Kelpies, straw hats, squeak of the plague cart,
The broadcasting van is wired to your heart —

No chance for the Shining One to show a snap
Of the one person you love, no late pass
Could get you back to Pleasure Pale, the train
Over the Divide has entered Cancel Cutting —
Ahead lie wheat plains in three-coloured clays,
Behind, the Fit City warm with mini-praise.

WHAT THE GUIDE BOOK SAID

Sited by gull course where the river swerves
    to fit a tendon of the Giant's Heel,
they laid logs to make a parallelogram
    and, balked of stone, from mud and wattle
built their church. St. Stephen-of-the-Surcingle
    was always holy : there the blessed Cunegonde
beheld the Virgin dreaming in a crystal,
    the scholar Timoleus waited for the call
to Rome. Fra Geronimo walked here
    with the last Margrave — they summoned
The Golden Age with twenty sheep deep grazing
    and a chaffinch picking at the crust of sky.
Soon the city boundaries hove in sight,
    the banished architect's bald cupola
flashed like a gold tooth in the morning sky;
    encroachment on these holy perches
was so quick, a brisk cockaded visitor
    was misdirected twice by citizens
on his pilgrimage. He came to hear
    the silver pornographer lecture
on the city's poet, the circle of Christ's world
    like St. Catherine's wheel turning
to light each face. Wars and quarrels
    lapped the low walls, working a patina
part smoke, part blood : at last the great exile
    rode here on a farting charger, portly
to his house's restoration — sullen chimes
    and lemon fire sat upon the Square of Penitents
and again before his adoring people he set
    the pose of copulation like a God.

SEAHORSES

When we were children
We would cheer to find a seahorse
Among the wrack the breakers lifted
On to the beach. Sometimes two or three were together,
A team to pull a chariot of cuttle,
Or like a suicide wreathed in fine
Sea ivy and bleached sea roses
One stiff but apologetic in its trance.
Seahorses were vikings;
Somewhere they impassively
Launched on garrulous currents
Seeking a far grave : wherever
That was, they set their stallion
Noses to it, ready to be garnered
In the sea's time at the sea's pleasure.
If we wondered why we loved them
We might have thought
They were the only creatures which had to die
Before we could see them —
In this early rule of death we'd recognise
The armorial pride of head, the unbending
Seriousness of small creatures,
Credit them with the sea's rare love
Which threw them to us in their beauty,
Unlike the vast and pitiable whale
Which must be quickly buried for its smell.

COMPETITION IS HEALTHY

Es wartet alles auf dich

Everything. Yes. Some men holy enough
To have seen the Buddha may try to keep
His commandments — to clothe the ragged in lightweight
Dacron, to feed the hungry with milk bread
Or curious corn, to press salve of the sacred
Laboratories of America into sores
Too big to form scabs. Yet the underprivileged
Rich pray for a Goldwater victory
Within an ant's tremor of God's instep.
Your heavenly Father knoweth that
Ye have need of all these things.
He gives bells that walk the fields
When the unsteady rice is shooting,
He gives Sebastian Bach to the citizens
Of Leipzig. Out of reach of the philharmonic
That old man is planting his garden.
He nestles each seedling in the soil,
Contrives a cotton grid to keep the sparrows off,
Sweats in conscience of his easy goal.
Unknown to him his son has scattered
Radish seed in the bed and the red clumsy
Tubers shall inherit the earth.
Take no thought saying ' What shall we eat?
What shall we drink? or Wherewithal shall we be clothed? '
We shall eat the people we love,
We shall drink their fluids unslaked,
We shall dress in the flannel of their blood,
But we shall not go hungry or thirsty
Or cold. The old man writes with a post office nib
To his son. ' The Government has cut the quotas,
Here the bougainvillea is out,
The imported rose is sinking in the heat.'

STEPS ON THE WAY

Brought down from the organ loft six books
Landscape-shaped, the Tables of the Law,
Sullenly finding all the greatness out,
Otherwise talking only to the school cooks,
Peeling onions without crying, a bore
To everyone : mother mad, father devout.

Seven years on, Cousin Thomas reports that
You've just been voted Student of the Year,
At Carnival seduce a Professor's wife,
Jeer at your friend ' old gargle-orgel, cat-
arse cantor ', pay for everyone's beer
With your idiot mother's savings. The toast is life.

You disappear. High in the oberland
A somewhat old pharmacy apprentice
On a cold day lies in a field with cows.
' The boat on Galilee rests now on warm sand
And there steps ashore a God. From this
Moment the larks starve which follow the ploughs.'

The Colonel-General offers you a smoke —
On your chest a small cross speaks black courage —
You must lead the Circus now, the Baron's dead.
A letter says poor Orgel's had a stroke :
They've smuggled in La Malandrine, the stage
Can lend her for a night to grace your bed.

Ten thousand unemployed are rioting
The night your viola concerto's premiered.
The light of diamonds speaks to your pale wits.
' I saw the host that sat and heard the king
Speak to them on death. We will not be spared,
Our country's a cold whore, a Gräfenitz.'

The town's on fire. The bombers will return.
A priest brings round the late-night watered milk.
The asylum clock ticks plainly in the dark.
' This is the sermon. Until our bodies burn
God can't see us.' In your last silk
Shirt by bomb light you are fingering Bach.

THE NEXT HUNDRED YEARS
WILL BE RELIGIOUS

Sticky from repairing his seventh vase,
Mr. Spark calls for hose joints and the smell

Of lilies of the valley. You know what
The great hunchback philosopher said,

This is an age of religion. Interpret it with flowers.
There is the first pansy my green hands

Ever trained to set down rated roots.
From the verandah the sun casts inch-long

Shadows, we are so close to twelve.
The milk of poinsettias makes rubber

On my palms. Keeping to great quantities,
I see no reason to think ill of things.

For a start more people are happy than
Ever were before. More are born whole, and

If out of the corner of your eye you see
Poor Stamp, thirty-five and of no

Definite sex, think how we set him off.
Our normality fills his nostrils like

Pollen. Poor chap, they say the bees kill
Their freaks. He lifts his head and feels

Pity peppering his nose : he smiles, he thinks
Humanists are lovely from the south,

He must feel grateful for perspectives,
His body leaks into his mind. In the drift

Of blossom over the window sill
He identifies the tower of history

Long on the slack land, queened by canals
And college grass — the wind lifts his eye

To a duckling train of monks smoking out
Devils from an innocent piece of death,

Up then to the corpse clouds whose light
Applauds two tears — somewhere else

In this unjust landscape a donkey takes
Two steps forward raising water in an old bucket,

The wheel moves a broken spoke a perfect circle,
The set bee moves through its archipelago,

Beside the A.A. box in dusty nettles
A dog leaps a dog and finishes too soon.

THE RETURN OF
INSPECTOR CHRISTOPHER SMART

There was, there really was a time on Galilee
Our Lord distrusted the lake weed, the little
liver-leaved plant with the speck of gold,
and Him the one that put the clothes on God —
consider the lilies and the talcum of the field,
these are the munitions of his majesty;
a top product like that needs marketing
so his strategy was bold : get the kids to want it —
those manic little bonbons on a stalk
ate the fat ears in the bugles of wheat,
they're blowing under the hill till resurrection,
they seed for Heaven; see the innocent eye
wait on them with names, stinking roger,
pee-the-bed, old man's balls — they praise
The Biggest Seedsman of them all, His beds of glass
shine past all the railway lines in Surrey !

This is just the start. It's wonderful to be back
with twenty thousand of you here tonight
Earls Court up in my spiel. I know you're waiting
to hear Avro Manhattan on the trombone
and the John Knox Chorale rendering
that mighty number ' Brays the Lord and Parse
the Admonition '.
                          Lie quiet James Joyce,
we're all Protestant spies here — wait till they've got
pessaries in the medicine cabinets in all the bathrooms
in Salamanca and the pill in a twist of blue
paper in every packet of Pacelli's Crisps
(that's how I like my Jews, he said, done to a crisp).
They've taken it all in their stride — Hildebrand,
sodomy, Luther, Pio Nono, Pacem in Terris,
they'll handle a bit of campus rut
in the Catholic West. Listen to that Vatican PR
' even when our boys sniffed that A-rab tail
in Aleppo, we could still get every man Bohemond

of them on parade if Christendom was growling.
Just now we're on a Management Consultant kick
but it's the Reader's Digest to last month's Mind
things have never been so jammy in Stateside
Outremer '
       So I remind you, don't underestimate
the Papists. Here's a few hints to fix your catholic
friends. Show them that book of Fulton Sheen
demonstrating the Mass : if they're intellectuals
that profile should do for them. And for the trogs,
send a list of seventy avant-garde poets
from the Tea House of the August Moon, all of whom
are secret catholics (put in a picture of
Thomas Merton playing backgammon with the editor
of Fortune). For my grounds in New Canaan
shall infinitely compensate for the flats and maynes
of Staindrop Moor. Coming under the hammer
at Sotheby's, Maureen Connolly's copy of the Little Flowers
with notes on the Adversary's backhand sweep.

But I digress, friends, and out of the mouth
of a pun comes the stalling truth. How, in fact,
do you die? Die well, die old, die howling,
die drunk, Dai Jenkins? I've talked to you
about life and other such old hat and a pretty
sad sight it looks, just like last week's
Colour Supplement. But what is life but the new
Unit Trust for Death? That's what we're getting ready for.
Watch for it in Monday's Newcomers. What is it
leads you beyond micro-skirts to the underside
of a cowrie?
       Back to the Wound.
          Back to God.
Your mother's lips as she squeezes on a peach
in her sunmilked kitchen and the tradespeople
at the backdoor taking bets on the afternoon meeting;
little Marie under the steps among the passionfruit
showing her Junior Chamber of Commerce, the wet
wide lick of the alsatian, the one leaf on the goldfish pond

coming round for the last time, manna from
the everlasting backyard, quails for grails,
hot corrugated iron on your backside and
erections receiving Heaven — the fingers climb
the scala peccatorum to the enskied Marina
where it's always soda time and the God-girls
in their yachting caps are willing. Miss Death's
got a cold in her whiskers and now the pilgrims
swarm to that sad spot. I left my crutches by her grotto,
carried her holy picture through the streets :
For I have seen the White Raven & Thomas Hall
of Willingham & am myself a greater curiosity
than both. If you're drowning those two puppies,
miss, I'll have the one with the pink nose.

So, you're going to die. What about HIM then?
I mean that one, der geist der stets verneint
(German's the only language I like to quote in)
The Adversary, the Accuser who is judge of this world.
There's a dead God if ever I saw one, a sort
of Nietzsche with the ichor drying on his arms
beside the duckboards the first day of Passchendaele.
He's your Uncle Mick that rested his big hams
on you by the ivy wall and talked of a fat man's love :
the Devil's the sun and this puppy world
has its tongue out, lap, lap ! Parry the Adversary
and believe in death.
                              You've got the scene,
we're bursting out of our budget in one of those city states,
the organiser from Romagna has got the boys
on the floats, they're enacting the Battle of Salamis
and the banks are lined with Master Botticelli's
' won't-melt-in-your-mouth ' girls, their hands
down the apprentices' fronts. Festina Lente !
Pico and Ficino are chatting up an old rabbi
with goose fat stains on his gaberdine,
time is burning in the ladies' cheeks,
the siege machines are rumbling through the celery
and where is il popolo grasso ? Taking a holiday
from cancer at the end of a Spanish pike.

Death is like this, a custom-built carnival
with the bill just about to be presented.
I see you as God sees you : one at a time, His
little Willy, daytime owl blinking at the light :
we've been Europeans now for a millenium
and where's it got us? Doing piece work
by strip lighting in Waco, Texas. It's the Anglo-Saxon's
privilege. He has his catacombs inside his head,
Rotarian dead to clap the dust he raises.
For the ENGLISH TONGUE shall be the language
of the WEST. *Dark Eyes Are Tracking Him* !
His epitaphs are polished on the moon.

AT THE THEATRE ON ST. VALENTINE'S EVE

Now the machines of art are more cunning
And the bar conversations more puerile.
Skill, great skill goes into the hair,
The tits, the teeth, the smiles, the heels.
We sit ranged in an hemisphere of dark
And the sun comes out on the stage. It's late
In our world, we cannot stand pain.
Though the author is ahead of us, we have
A sophistication better than his words.
Having taken the graph of pain to the top
Of the paper, we rule new grids with love;
Why should the line ever stop? These sweet
Washed girls are virtuosi of light,
Mutants of harm are lovely and come to the call —
The West is washing its dirty linen in blood.

MOANING IN MIDSTREAM

You can see the Master's latch-key
at the University of Anaconda,
plus a note from a girl who wanted
to write poetry (' I feel vowels like peaches '),
the picture he bought at the Salon —
' Sardanapalus Prepares for Death ' —
and several letters to a Normandy vet
about boarding out his dog.
I looked in one hot day in June
before rehearsing my Organa
for Thirteen Orchestras. Lucky Master,
I thought, living at the doomed end
of a serious century, and went off
to hear Knipper's Concerto for Farts.
But there in the library gloom go
the dark geniuses, dapper and intense
in their fin de siècle silences,
caught by the camera ridiculously
at Seine boating parties, or heavy-glanded
watching balloons go up : arrogant,
incurable, hell in the home —
No point in regretting them or lauding
their relics : still, how nice just
not to be here at the fifth concert
of the series, trying hard to be fair, trying
harder still to like something, feeling
only breath won too easily on closed faces.

THE ECLIPSE OF LADY SILVERTAIL

Baffled by clarity, her last victims
Stare at us from library books,
Donizetti's fevers and syrup of digitalis,
Wolf's mask of rest at the end
Of a screaming century. Watch by
Your brother's bed for copy, the end
Of a man may have the most artistry.
It's all public now : never more
The spent genius wrapped in rugs
With mercury-blacked teeth, wheeled
To a yellow hedge, his amanuensis by.
The Lady's best incarnation was
A thin lighterman's daughter
Living ten summers down at
Teddington. She slipped a blessing
On a younger son for Calcutta's
Heat to hatch out. She was generous,
She sang. Little Lady Silvertail,
You whiten us by wish-light — fear
Of you is nesting in us still,
Up some worn steps we hope we never drag,
Some doctors' booming jokes
We'll never raise a laugh at —
We have a homage to pay to
Old daguerreotypes, to the eyes
Of Europe fallen in eclipse,
Noses pecked off out of empty air.

FUTURITY

If you could guess at seven
That the little girl with plaits
And the band on her teeth would be
Fata Morgana the great star and Alice
The most invited girl in the street
Would later turn her feast of eyes
On the recurring chianti bottles
Of the asylum wall paper
Counting forever up to ten
With no crack in the world to follow,
If Sophonisba with the spots
Playing Czerny in the sun
Through afternoons of talc and zinnias
Could guess to what use a half-moon
Carving knife might be put,
If Ralph the even-tempered Saxon
Who carried his bat through ten
Summers could prognosticate
His two children and the pulp
He'd make of their brains with a new
Tack hammer — if all these could
Then perhaps you could have seen
Standing beside the mossy overflow
Of the rain tank that your nerves'
Carnival would sink to a smile
From Bridget, to three children
And a clock of dead chimes, that and
A three inch par. in the local paper
When you saved an oiled seagull
From the Council boatshed, crying
And smiling for one death the less,
This strange fate of a tropical Nietzsche
Condemned to the Bizet of his dreams,
A silted sinus and two doctors
Casting short shadows on the lawn.

HOMILY IN THE ENGLISH READING ROOMS

The plains people never liked this place,
Trapped here by an ethnic kink,
Unable to get away after their Augustus
Corrected the boundaries. The river is deep
But the marshes are too wide and just
In the wrong place. That great bridge
Would look magnificent if it weren't
Coated half the year with primer — a day
After alighting at the cement-winged
Central Station you find yourself drinking
The sophisticated one of the three beers
At the very café a film made famous.
Coke is dear, so the locals drink it —
You sit at the Drei Sklaven and tell
Lies over the new wine. Around those smiles
There seems too much prosperity — haven't
These people suffered, where is the shadow
On the plate of their souls? Across the Square
In the ugly building where the Negro
Basketball team plays tonight, wasn't that
The scene of the great Saalschlacht?
It's been a cinema since and a repository.
Something makes you quarrelsome — one
Argues over a tram number, the other fails
To find a lavatory on the Kai, the first
Remarks that boxers outnumber dachshunds,
The second that water feels the same fine-blown
From council fountains the world over. When
Did brushed pigskin reach this part of the world?
That book *The World of the Stingray* upsets you;
Although all you can say in their language is
Your room number to the fat lady behind her paper
You resent the internationalism : at last,
Lying awake in one third of a hard bed,
The dark lapping your chin, the hot
Body beside you feeling for your nerves,
The lattice shows one or two stars, alien

Like you but professionally filled with light.
When the person you love is as strange to you
As the nervous system of the frog, you may,
If your fate holds, arrive one day
At the ultimate non-connection — a room
Over a baker's shop, the landlord's daughter
On the stairs with two hot rolls and a cup
Of coffee for your breakfast; then the shot
And your dead body on the seersucker quilt,
Nobody's business but the Vice-Consul's
And the police's; a beautiful change
Of the soul's weather while tours come south
Over the passes and the Grand Expatriate
Takes his morning drink with the Mayor's son
In the café Norman loved and talks
Of his Prep. School under a red umbrella.

THREE POEMS FOR MUSIC

(I)

A scandal is starting now,
look where Helen, shoulder-borne,
   teeters to the see-saw ships.

A well-paid Florentine saw this,
   a man in a soft collar
follows a girl to the next gallery.

(II)

A flayed skin keeps the features of a man,
   A star followed flushes out a God,
A foot in the ragged robin brings to land
   The Emperor's ship on his exiled shore,
A forgotten name bruises a girl's blood,
   The world waits for love to cast a claw.

(III)

Though this is not in Hesiod,
Music was stolen from a God :

Not fire but notes the primal giver
Paid for with helpings of his liver

And virtuosi of the earth
Outsang the Gods who gave them birth.

When Orpheus plays we meet Apollo,
When there's theology to swallow

We set it to music, our greatest art,
One that's both intellect *and* heart,

There war and peace alike depict us
(Drums and trumpets in the Benedictus) —

It sang beneath the Grecian boat,
It kept Pythagoras afloat,

It suffered poets, critics, chat
And will no doubt survive Darmstadt;

This brandy of the damned of course
To some is just a bottled sauce,

Its treasons, spoils and stratagems
Aleatory as women's hems

Yet beauty who indulged the swan
At death completes her with a song

And Paradise till we are there
Is in these measured lengths of air.

ST. CECILIA'S DAY, 1710

In memory of W. F. Bach

Having nothing new to say but born
    in the middle of a warm skill,
watching the animals of art
    grazing undisturbed as if
on the savannahs of the moon,
    free by virtue of failure
of the egregious disruptions
    of fashion, you are the star
to hail across centuries
    of competitive rubbish :
marked by the small beast's
    epiphany, worn by the stair lights
of princes, the clubbable season
    of shiny trousers awaits you,
a firework of freeloaders
    day tripping by the burghers' sea.

And this in your broad hat :
    the landladies are polishing
the black stained tables
    making a great ordinariness
which is like art; a light
    somewhere high on a buzz
of crotchets weans a face
    to misery : the milk of this world
boils over and a loved
    firstborn son arrives
on the planet death. We are all
    children lying awake
after the light is put out.

ST. CECILIA'S DAY EPIGRAMS

(I)

Beaten to work, Caliban roars
His resentment to the stone ears
Of the hills, from whose magic hollows
A separate music blandly flows.
Energy is conserved : each sound he vents
Sets twangling that thousand instruments.

(II)

Annotators agree Composer X
Though always in love never had sex,

While a thousand motets and masses lie
To the credit of sex-mad Composer Y,

And that lover of life, Composer Z
In his operas wishes he were dead.

Each in his paradoxical way
Does a lot for the famous Critic K.

ONE DIED IN METAPHOR AND ONE IN SONG

Meridian fixed to walk out on death's crutches.
His hobbling made many fears dance : a vicar
Saw God melt into midday; short Mosaic law
Was ironed to ruin a man in print.
It came out straight, lines that didn't meet.
They make a grill for loneliness. Once bent,
The fire passes, the metal holds its shape —
Calm governors wonder at a world of wretches,
Healed liberals have read it all before,
Our darkness shows the exodus of heat.

Parallel went mad, lived thirty years
Devising antiphons and metric for the Psalms,
Put Mrs. Perkins with her rose red hands
Through Job's afflictions : his cat received
A dictat playing with a mouse; God did this
While growling at raw meat. Then one laved
Skin made equatorial by sex,
Saw sin enfranchised in his spiralling hairs :
All Brunel's steam and spit of Freikorps bands
Only amplifies the hush of Genesis.

WHY WE GET DRUNK

Pestered by wives and bells,
   Hiccuping regrets, we
Try to get these sulphur songs
   By heart to sing them
To smilers on the terraces
   And pallid experts
Who know how much of the moon
   Is rich in nitrate.
A useless pilgrimage and one
   To die on early.
Nice to be looking upwards
   When the blow falls, have
No name, no friends, no luck.
   How does this differ
From a gregarious face
   Stopped in the mirror
Waiting tidily for pain?

PIG IN THE MIDDLE

(The Daily Express — Friday, November 15th, 1963)

Wallowing in luxury lay
A Most Important Pig —
Cornelius, Top Pig of the Year —
Pink and White, bacon-rich Cornelius!
Where a couple of weeks ago lissom young ladies
Were competing for Miss World,
Cornelius basked under camera lights
Like an odalisque in a Turkish harem.
' What a clean pig ', we all exclaimed.
' O very clean ', they answered, ' we washed him
For his debut in detergent '.
Cornelius is the first M.D.H.
(Minimal Disease Hybrid).
Fat and fancy Cornelius grew to bacon-
slicing size in only one hundred and twenty-nine days.
He derives from high-bred Landrace
And Large White parents. He wasn't born,
He was removed from his mother by hysterectomy.
His upbringing (bottlefed with a minutely balanced diet)
Ensured against infections which pigs are prone to
From the moment of his birth.
His cereal and fish-meal feed
Was carefully tinctured
With chalk, copper, zinc, molybdenum and other minerals.
For every $2\frac{1}{2}$ pounds of food he ate
He put on more than a pound in weight.
But what about flavour?
Age and exercise put flavour into meat,
But the hard facts of farm economics
And a reasonable price for the housewife
Means animals must be grown fast and killed young.
Poor Cornelius!
He is the only pig that ever wallowed
In Waldorf luxury.
His debut in the Aldwych Suite cost £50,
All to make a better British breakfast.

THE RECIPE

Smelling of love like a piece
of oiled wood, I shaded
those bleached shores.

Pull back the sun under your belt
I said. An old lady is mad
among staghorns and potted maidenhair,
her family were sugar boilers of Huguenot stock;
now they have refined themselves away.

A new land has ghosts waiting
at the mangrove quays.
The journeys are all inland.

Ambushed by those little migrant eyes.

Baptised in their bellies, the sun men
strapped the country to their backs.
' Pendragon, Belinda and Jack, March '65 '.

These are the wrong ingredients.

Take instead a veined and freckled man
with his ten year old son
treading among the uguary shells
talking about the world's drawn blinds,
the boarding house of hell where meals are prompt.
Europe has tipped these workings
on a spastic shore.
A dredge is called the Dauntless
and a road that runs nowhere
is named after the native pubis.

It was breadfruit in the books
and bread deliveries in the street.

The milkshakes are pouring
for the matutinal mass :
in the cool of the bush house
bulldog ants are rebuilding the republic.
On her ninetieth birthday Aunt Blin
thanks the cousins for their present of death.

When we're strong enough we'll make them call
this north and Europe south.

A picture of Ayers Rock was given to
everybody at the Press Reception.

I bless my ancestors in the name
of the cornucopia and the gibber plains.

FIVE GENERATIONS

A common name for five of us
tap-rooted to the world's work;
we are the unknown bearers,
the wearers of fatty uniforms.

But only five? Where I'm writing
men of one name have lived in one place
for three hundred years. Our family's modern,
moving out of historic darkness
in a diaspora of the undistinguished.

Christopher Porter starts from the dark —
I wouldn't pay to trace him farther back,
I simply put him down as something in the town,
the town a sprawling somewhere stealing
a march upon the pelting countryside.
In the blackening days of Captain Swing
for some unmentioned tic of change
he sailed for New South Wales. I see him
walking the deck to escape his wife,

donating a spit to Liverpool in his wake :
too cold a man to care what lies ahead
he takes an unimportant step from England's shadow.

Robert, his son, is different. An enema'd Victorian,
Master Builder of a pushing city,
he went up spires of speculation
breathing port and senna, was prig enough
to put his money into banking : the brewery
he wouldn't back is worth a million now.
Family legend says he entertained
Trollope but never saw a kangaroo —
pride did what cupidity could not
and he lost his money — unbending
in late madness, he fulminated
through maidenhair, berated crotons,

killed ants by matchlight in his bush house.
He built Brisbane's gaol and deep water pier
and was hated by a little boy, my father.
When Robert cried the flood of '93 began;
the little boy whistling at his birds
lived with a mad god. Thereinafter
he broke his traps and read
the small print on council bye-laws.

Frederick, my grandfather, filled his house
with pictures of ' the *Thermopylae* doing eight knots
in a breeze that wouldn't blow a candle out '.
He looked like Bernard Shaw and sat
stiff as a row of Georgette Heyers
navigating on green baize. He sailed
in his emptiness like a cloud, yet once
rode the Queensland customs boundary
never out of plumb upon his horse.
Over a steaming saddle of mutton his face
was a plastic monument to severity —
while he partitioned meat
the Congress of Vienna would have paused.
For love of him his daughter used herself,
a dowry of cancer being bait
no girl of fifty should lay out.
I remember the tepid lump of eucalyptus sugar
moving in his meccano fingers;
he became a place of work
and laboratory of a Yankee quack.

William's the good man of them all.
It hurts to think of that sandy shore
he loves, that bitumen and mangrove
bird house he must raise his voice in.
He's given eighty years of disenchanted
love to it : when he dies, they should
trawl him over river sand to Avalon
out of the choppy, bitching bay.

Peter from necessity cannot speak.
This crop of bones might tumble on his coffin
claiming its own. Death's a relation
waiting to get in touch. Born to that sad
reversal of light, he'll know
when to pull the blinds down and go home.

AN UNIMPORTANT TRAGEDY

Six hundred yards from the end
Of this barrel, hardly to be seen,
Obscured by a green dot which
Is a two foot wide lantana bush
Lies the target : a space between
Two red rocks. Foreshortened,
It has scant importance — the gun-
metal stays cool even in this heat —
Lining up the target properly
In the sights unaccountably draws
Attention to a white tree perhaps
Two hundred yards closer — that would
Be transparent gum on the bark,
A lizard scampering along a branch,
A dead patch at half past three —
Mistletoe ! Birds fly in its hair,
It's blazed for the Mission Station,
Reckless of floods that tyrannise
The valley. From the tree a wire
Straggles to the ground and leads
The eye to a water trough — the black
Does not mean the water's deep
But that algae, wrigglers and moss
Have thickened the dark — the flash
Of fire from one end is the sun
Slipping on a not yet rusted tin;
There is the castaway carton
With the three X stencil, erupted
Of its beer; back on short tape
To the target the only prominence
Is a cairn of rocks, obviously
The grave of a dog, a blue kelpie,
Now a skeleton from tunnelling
Ants; under the hundredweights
Of stones a memorial of death
The general country will incline to.
Space between the rocks behind

The green dot darkens, then the will
Sets the trigger on, the sound of
The shot bounds up the valley —
A man falls small and for
A second dustily on a space
Of plain earth at the six hundred
Yard point from this cool gun.
Just a clean shot that might be
Justice or murder or insanity
But has anyway from the vantage
Of this steering barrel presented
A new object to a not very cluttered
River floor, one that might come
To interest the birds in the tree or
The dead dog's ants or some men
Coming up the valley with
Texts and vows and explanations.

FAIR GO FOR ANGLO-SAXONS

(A near-contemporary gallimaufry)

(1)

Provincial Messiah

To be under thirty
and already have written ten pronunciamenti,
to think all older writers
only want to lay you
and boast of the girls you've laid,
to think no-one is any good
except a poet from Alberta,
Catullus and some friends
who run a mimeographed magazine,
to misquote Ovid, misrepresent Pound,
misunderstand Olson and never
have heard of Edwin Arlington Robinson,
to have to print your girl friend's
things alongside your own,

to be all this is better
than to have talent and have to write well.

(2)

At the Trat'

The translator of aphorisms
is wining and dining the actress/playwright/
wife of the famous TV Producer.
Everyone in the restaurant, including
the determined client-suitors,
is eavesdropping now. Red wine
and vintage sex life spill among
Sicilian smiles. She's an old hand —
she can stick to Lichtenberg
and the hundred German devils

while he gets a feel in.
The waiters are sending money home.
Now says Old Ruby Nose topping up his glass
the goat-faced youth are knocking up the girls
in the randy grass of Agrigentum.
In her next play she retells the story
of Persephone : we winter with her
as she greets the God in jeans.

(3)

Sibylline Stutterings

After the New Emancipation
The New Rudeness,
After the New Heterosexuality
The New Cruelty,
After the New Live Art
The New Messiahs,
After the New Violence
The New Dandyism,
After the New Controversy
The New In-Touchness,
After the New Complexity
The New Indeterminacy,
After the New Toughness
The New Lyricism,
After the New Expressionism
The New Communication,
After the New Concern
The New Loneliness.

(4)

Lines

She's loyal to the marmalade she bought in Danzig
They found paddi-pads in the Chairman's trunks
Boethius or Bride to the Thing in the Box : two good reads

Wise old eyes have perused the small print
He told her he didn't love her in the Restful Tray
Proof of genius : fatty degeneration of the heart
She was buried holding her Tolkien books
Sunday and the fish are parsing the reviews
O for Pauline in the french nylon knickers
So neighbourly, a candid Canuck and a smiling Finn
God died underfoot — in the steps of the master
Köchel, even the fifth edition notwithstanding, the score
includes bassoons
The comic novelists' convention is ending

(5)

Twenty-four lines

A common cold wins
provinces for a man,
an arbiter of elegance
rides into town on a Bactrian camel

The ravines of this city
are full of gold and milkshakes :
a light box where the pain shows up,
I mean the world, our clean small world

Face to face with wise Inquisitors
I tore my skin in night despair,
I am the Quinbus Flestrin
of this louche Lilliput

A lot of religious black men
strip the air of its European clothes,
the occupying army leaves behind
a complete set of the Waverley Novels

Can you solve the problem
of the Pervigilium Veneris
or graft the Peace Rose
on the Lady Buchanan?

The forks are shut up in the drawer,
the word has come among us —
I that in health was and . . .
wounds healed forever leave a scar.

(6)

Festina Lente

A slowing heart behind a whitening face —
    Death is going faster.
9 a.m. till noon, new International Master
    Class : time, action, space —
Music is made as the Rabbi made bread,
    Leaving fire to Heaven.
The slave's hatred is necessary leaven,
    The real slave's the egg-head.

Man is born free but is everywhere in chains,
    To them he owes his art.
The Rules Man gets off to a flying start,
    He knows the twisting lanes.
The Freedom Man has a million winning posts,
    He pays on every starter —
There on Tomorrow's Campus the living martyr
    Sniffs at the farts of ghosts.

(7)

Porter's Metamorphoses

Fishy,
thirteen year old Willesden born schoolgirl model
protegée of Godefroid de Bouillon
        (né Blinks)
is found one morning turned into
an embroidered Victorian altar cloth
in Siddal's Resurrection Rooms.

Jocelyn Brouha,
Wykehamist Accounts Executive,
deviser of award-winning bra campaigns
and originator of the slogan ' Tat for Tit ',
is reconstituted as page 257
of the Penguin edition
of the Annotated Elinor Glyn.

Ambrose Smilo
is made Ambrose Smilo
to the delight of six continents
and the G.P.O.

Martin Seymour-Smith
by a costive diet of integrity,
a perilous run of rule breaking
and through extravagant over-exposure
to the demands of friendship
is turned into a Soho pub clock
and forced to show
closing time forever.

Simon Puer
while chatting up a critic
at the Festival Hall bar
sees himself fade
to a smile on the face
of Alexander Goehr.

' Basic English ',
the psychedelic pop group
appearing as usual with erections
in Augsburg armoured codpieces
becomes the 1875 frieze
' The Triumph of Pan '
by O. D. Acres on the Winter Garden Theatre,
Mudland-juxta-Mare.

Arsehole,
wonder horse,
eats his get-well cards
in full view of the Television cameras :
later he is found
reading Gulliver's Travels
in the office of the Director General
of the **B.B.C.**

Four Soho poets
find themselves able
to pay their taxi fare home.
From shame they change
into mutton-chop whiskered
sidesmen at St. Vedast's
in the year of the Durbar.

En route to the Out Patients Dept.,
a scorching article
on five elder poets in his pocket
under his favourite pseudonym,
Ian Hamilton
is side-tracked to Madame Tussaud's
and melted down
for their new tableau
' The Suicide of Hart Crane '.

Playing the first of the " 48 "
on his Bermondsey gas pipe
didgeree-du, Wolfe Morris,
becomes ' The Wanderer's Pozzie '
motel at Surfer's Paradise
on the Gold Coast, near Brisbane,
Queensland, Australia.

Christopher Columbus,
for turning back at landfall
Hispaniola,
in reward for not discovering America
is elected Pope Urban XIX
and publishes the first
bull on contraception,
' De Temporibus Tutis '.

(8)

Half-Mast Poems

The quick brown fox jumped over
    the lazy dog. The M.F.H.
had been up typing all night.

Open the window and let it in
    said the parson. I want a terror
applicable to my Sunday sermon.

Oxford Marmalade is American owned.
    Ten public-spirited Coopers
resign from the Telephone Directory.

The pollen count in London was 107.
    That was the day he caught the Speaker's eye
In the Westminster Public Convenience.

Now for the great work, begun among the ruins
    of Western Civilisation, the start of the long return,
this morning in the A.B.C. in Westbourne Grove. . . .

Two Nations!
The Rich and the Poor, the South and the North?
No, the Attractive and the Unattractive.

THE PORTER SONG BOOK

(I)

(Wir haben beide lange zeit geschwiegen)

We sit untalkative in a room
The light is leaving : after such words
The flesh cannot get close enough
To hold half-smiles. Love's angel
Will not come; the warm world
Of lime trees, madness and
Pianoforte albums has given way
To goadings in the yellow gloom
Of Gospel Oak. The silence after love
Is broken, not by the closing wings
Of the Nineteenth Century, but by
An article on topless dresses
Tossed into stale air. This severity
Is just to vex. From the fenced wood
A black spirit flaps up to our eaves.

(II)

Story from a Travel Book

They spent three months in the marshes.
Love and the water turned them into
Beautiful animals. They told their rescuers
The wide Delta sun steamed up
Like a river boat, each of them became
A soothsayer, sounds of struck brass
Were lost in the flattened reeds.
There was one death — baked in golden mud
He lay among a childish people
Caressed by keening. One great soul
Saw the light go out, reached for
The Akkadian dark : smelling a little of urine,
He was taking one step on to the stars

When a French engineer found him,
Blue-eyed, still recognisably European,
But suffering from malnutrition that
No river dog or girl of twelve
Could be companion to or compensate.

(III)

The Sanatorium

Flowers brought by the lying woman
Break from bud and sweep the room,
But die rightly with the scent gone.
By coughing light she comes, telling
Stories of childhood, of the long
Verandahs and the travelling aunts.
To the doctor she speaks of being
With him on his Magic Mountain,
For the man she wishes a mind
Not easily frightened by Managing
Directors' parables. Like lonely
Hangers in hotel wardrobes they rock
Occasionally at doors opening :
Turning his eyes to her, he sees
A wall without bricks lit
By endless sunshine brightening.

(IV)

Clairvoyant

You've narrowed the horizon to a noose
And in anxiety bang about the house,
The enemy of vases. One or two people,
Your husband for a start, will die
When eventually they get past you
To the disneyland inside your head.
You're a spiky girl the children love,
You always settle with the milkman early;
But still you gaze through lines and dream

Of living : here is peace, the reach
Of an old river with lawns to its edge
And an opposite bank nobody has seen.

(V)

Journal Entry

Then when we stop the car deep in cow parsley
And strive against the epitaphs of love,
There comes a minute of peace — back to back
Hands pressed against our forheads, we
Keep to the shallow end of shadows, not
Needing to think about the quick-built walls,
Guards with their backs turned or playground
Sand scattered to cover up our blood.

(VI)

Genius Loci

Look, nothing has changed —
the great spoor have never faded,
the jugular tips blood from a new quarry,
there is a parting by an iron fountain,
rays of water fan from the sun of this place
and there in his accustomed corner
sits nature's godson,
nursing his face on the water's skin.
Do not come, love, if you are afraid
to turn into a barbered shrub :
what we are now the fire will hold.

(VII)

In Hora Ultima

At the final hour
Everything will be destroyed —

The trumpet's steel and silver throat,
The plated flute's garden note,
The plucking at the pelvis of the lute;
Waltzers of the Middle World
Shall turn no more,
The great bassoon joke
Die on the German tongue,
The émigré dancer leap
Beyond the compass of his mind.
This is when the one tune plays
Which only death sings descant to.

(VIII)

The Visitation

A night after Michaelmas, under
   The no-light of sodium, I
Foxed and sniffed at the stippled glass
   Of her door and scratched
With my claws for her. She had
   Kissed these tomb-robber's hands,
And now the pictured girl implored
   The god of the dead to find her.
Watching through the glass, I waited
   Her emboldened coming down
The carpeted hall, her body
   Like a document held out,
Night cream shining on her face.

(IX)

Lyric found in a bottle

I'm locked in my own body.
Today I found a small worm
In the wood of my heart. Now
I'll push it through the bars
To freedom. Perhaps if you see

A crushed worm on the path
You will visit me. The words
I write are delicate :
Straighten these serifs of pain
And I will feel your body
Along their line. I'm your worm
Of love, I'm working towards
You in the sun : look down,
The land shines where I crawl.

(X)

Late Lyric

An area one inch by about
Three inches of his left arm
Is heated by the sun. Warming his nose,
He bends to kiss her in the sun.
An area one inch by about
Three inches of her left cheek
Is heated by the kiss.
She stretches out an arm from infinity
To take him apart,
Till he is one inch by about
Three inches of wetness on the skirt
And curtain of her perfect love.

(XI)

Poetry

An old art spreading rumours about
Paradise, it begs outside the gates
Of the gods : the active gods come out.

(XII)

White Wedding

At St. Columba's or St. James's, Spanish Place,
Before a congregation freezing in
Quant and quantities of ice and lace
Two butterflies are waiting for the pin.
The organ loft is stuffed with violins,
The pipes ascend to Heaven; they want to roar,
But do not give the cue for Mendelssohn,
See the bride's eyes are filled with tears and sore
With looking at the groom's dynastic nose.
Alas, alas, God's rosters are declared,
Tears dry quickly fanned by Prayer Book prose,
If love can't be, then hatred may be shared.

(XIII)

The mynah bird dips its beak
In the friendly man's pale beer,
Three salesmen talk of their careers,
Two feet play hide and seek.

The bird says suddenly ' dirty old man '.
I look at my finger nails — dirt !
I'm 35, half the Psalmist's span;
If I took off my clean shirt

I'd stand before you pilled in fat.
Each day I clean the floor of my cage,
The body smells more at my age,
The words of love come pat.

(XIV)

From an Old Master

On the green cloth of summer lie
Bullrushes, water, ducks and sky.
There Christ, a sinless silver boy,
In his mother's lap sits like a toy;
A sapling lapped in pale green moss
Casts down the shadow of the Cross.

(XV)

Quick Frozen Poem

God, she's wolfed two sides
    of gold-grained plaice.
    From that small fish and loaves
    we fed a multitude.

    My need is straightforward now,
     another pun to go on with :
    Of her bones are quarrels made.

God, let me die of it
    only with a temperature
    and violent telegrams.

(XVI)

One . two . . three . . . lyric

Wheel switch smoke Donne eye hand rub
Lie wall black wide no and yes
Now now mark sit right laugh pub
Road owl sweet have teach tail love.

Repton Beddoes bauxite city
Punch-up Collect clock-golf Waldsee

Slipped disc planchette merger Korngold
Set dream spasm Coulsdon money.

Dorset Church Chaney's eyes Daddy's step Mummy's breath
Kattomeat nine nineteen Engadine Book of Hours
Copy Chief cattle truck L S D Head of Seth
Dry ice burn garden dig world without end in death.